To Deb
My Soul Mate
in Garlic
Love,
Marilyn
1991

THE
LITTLE GARLIC
BOOK

Rosamond Richardson

St. Martin's Press
New York

Drawings by Linda Broad.
Designed by Ken Leeder.
Cover photograph by John Lee.

Library of Congress Cataloging in Publication Data

Richardson, Rosamond.
    The little garlic book.

    I. Cookery (Garlic) 2. Garlic I. Doeser, Linda.
    II. Berriedale-Johnson, Michelle. III. Title
TX819.G3D63 1983   641.6′526   83-2884
ISBN 0-312-48864-5

First U.S. Edition

10 9 8 7 6 5 4 3 2 1

First published in Great Britain by Judy Piatkus (Publishers)
Limited.

Contents

GARLIC – THE PLANT

People either love garlic or they hate it. Most people love it — and everyone feels strongly about it. Garlic is one of the oldest cultivated plants in existence and it has been flavouring our food and curing our ills from mythological times. The plant is native to central Asia, where it grows wild, and because of its immense popularity it has been introduced into warm sunny climates all over the world.

Garlic is a perennial or biennial herb, and its bulb possesses anti-bacterial properties. It is a member of the lily family (Liliaceae) and a relative of onions and chives, of the autumn crocus or meadow saffron, of the bluebell and of the lily of the valley. The botanical name of the cultivated variety is *Allium sativum*.

The bulb which develops just beneath the surface of the soil consists of between 8 and 20 cloves, and each clove is enclosed in a papery, slightly silky, skin. The skin is usually white, but can be pinkish or even mauve. All parts of the plant are strongly scented, but the bulb smells the most pungent. The flavour of the cloves develops best in the sun; if the bulb gets cold or wet, the cloves taste acrid and smell rank.

The plant grows best in rich, light and well-drained soils, and it can grow to between 1 and 3 feet high. It has a straight, unbranched stem and several erect, long and pointed leaves which, unlike those of its cousin the chive, are not hollow but flat. The leaves of both the wild and the cultivated varieties can be chopped up and added to salads. The flavour of the leaves is somewhat milder than that of the bulb and they make a nice change from chives.

The flowers, which appear in July and August, are densely packed together to form a clump or 'umbel'. The little flowers are usually white, tinged with green or light purple. A characteristic of garlic is that the flower stalks bear tiny bulbs, which are called bulblets or bulbils, instead of seeds. The flavour of the bulbils is as strong as that of the cloves and they can be used in cooking.

Garlic grows wild in Britain but the bulbs are too small to be used in the kitchen. Those to be found in the wild are *A. ursinum*, Ramsons or Bear's garlic; *A. vineale*, Crow garlic; *A. oleraceum*, Field garlic; *A. ampeloprasum*, Wild leek and its variation holmense, Great-headed garlic; and *A. scorodoprasum*, Sand leek. *A. canadense* is Canadian garlic, and *A. chinense* is cultivated in China and Japan where they call it Rakkyo. One beauty which has been selected for garden cultivation is *A. moly*, Golden garlic, a native of southern Europe. It stands 12 inches tall, has lance-shaped leaves and its bright yellow star-shaped flowers growing in umbels well merit it a place in the herbaceous border. Another one to grow in your garden for its decorative white starry flowers is *A. tuberosum*, Chinese chives.

Garlic is prone to several pests and diseases, among which are the stem-eelworm, the bulb-eelworm, thrips, white rot and other virus ailments. White rot causes the base of the bulb to be covered with a white fluffy fungal growth, and it causes the leaves to yellow and die back.

Surprisingly, garlic makes a good companion plant. Carrots thrive when planted next to garlic, and when planted next to roses, as the garlic grows any blackspot on the roses will disappear. It is said that the garlic actually enhances the perfume of the rose, because the rose, provoked by its reeking competitor, will manufacture more scent! Believe that if you like. However, garlic can be made into a disinfectant which is an effective pesticide for the onion-fly that afflicts raspberries and grapes, and also kills mosquitoes, aphids, houseflies and the cabbage white butterfly.

COUNTRY NAMES
FOR GARLIC

G arlic (*Allium sativum*) gets its common name from the Old English 'garleac'. 'Gar' was a spear or lance, and thus describes the shape either of the stem of the garlic or the leaves; 'leac' is leek, a pot-herb or vegetable. *Allium* is of obscure derivation, but possibly comes from the Celtic 'all' which means pungent. *Sativum* means wild.

Common or local names for garlic include Poor Man's Treacle or Triacle, Devil's Posy, Witch Poison, Camphor of the Poor, and Food of Love.

In French garlic is *ail*, in German *knoblauch*, in Spanish *ajo*, and in Italian *aglio*.

POOR MAN'S TREACLE OR TRIACLE

Both these names come from a Greek word for 'antidote', for which the Latin was *thieracus*. This word was corrupted to become 'triacle', and thence 'treacle'. Garlic certainly fulfilled the role of poor man's antidote — for centuries man used plants both wild and cultivated as his medicine cupboard.

DEVIL'S POSY

Garlic must have got this country name from the widely held superstition that garlic is an infallible protection against evil. It was thought that the devil and all his works would be foiled if you held garlic in your hand.

WITCH POISON

Garlic was inimical to witches too; it was so potent that their antics and mischievous doings were rendered powerless if garlic were growing nearby.

CAMPHOR OF THE POOR

This is a derogatory title. Garlic's reputation has taken punishment periodically throughout its history, and at certain times it was regarded as peasant food, vile and stinking, with a smell as pungent as camphor and fit only for those who could afford nothing better.

FOOD OF LOVE

Garlic undermined Circe's plans entirely: not only did her potions not work on the garlicky Odysseus as she tried to turn him into swine along with his companions, but it also made her fall completely in love with him. Garlic thus acquired the reputation of being an aphrodisiac.

HOW TO GROW GARLIC

One of the best varieties of garlic to grow success-
fully is the large-cloved garlic from Clermont-
Ferrand in the Massif Central of France. It likes the
rugged climate and conditions and produces large
healthy bulbs. Large cloves usually yield a cluster of
large bulbs, but small inner cloves sometimes only
produce a single bulb. There is also evidence to prove
that cloves planted before the end of the year will
produce bigger bulbs than those planted in spring, so
November is the ideal month for planting.

Start by dividing a head of garlic into cloves,
making sure that every one is firm to the touch and
undamaged, and leave them unpeeled. Choose the
largest cloves and plant them with the pointed end
up, 1½ inches deep and 6 inches apart. The soil
should be light, rich and well drained, and the
position sunny. Garlic can also be grown in pots and
windowboxes, using garden soil or potting compost,
provided the drainage is good.

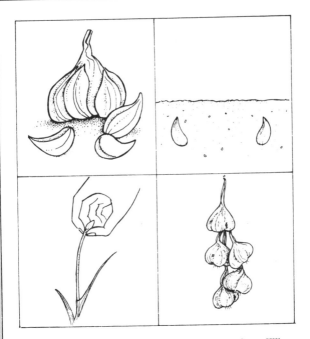

Keep the bulbs well-watered and weed-free. When the plants flower in the summer, nip off the heads to keep the best of the flavour in the bulb. When the tops start yellowing and dying back in late July and August, the crop is ready for harvesting.

Lift the bulbs carefully, for they bruise easily. Cut off the roots and tops and lay them on racks, or hang them up by their flower-stalks, to dry off either in the sun — if you're lucky enough — or in a cool dry airy place.

STORING GARLIC

Keep garlic in a dry place where it is not touching other vegetables, otherwise it will rot. The cloves tend to sprout if they are stored at temperatures over 70°F (20°C), and a bluish-green mould may appear when the relative humidity is greater than 70%. The ideal arrangement is to hang the bulbs up so that air can circulate around them. You can buy wire garlic baskets which serve this purpose.

Whole cloves are odourless, so they can be hung in a kitchen with no fear of pollution. Garlic only smells when it is crushed or bruised. This is due to enzyme activity which releases allicin, the substance that gives garlic its characteristic smell.

The French traditionally plait up the leaves of garlic to make garlic strings (as they make onion strings) and these are sold to the housewife. The plaits look most attractive hanging in the kitchen, and the bulbs keep for many months. The average length of a string of garlic is about 2 feet, but in the 'World's Longest Garlic Braid' competition held in California in 1981, the winner made a rope 63 feet long, made up of 1,450 garlic heads!

THE HISTORY OF GARLIC

G arlic has been cultivated in the East for centuries, and as early as 2000 BC the Chinese found it indispensable for both cooking and medicine. There are two essential ingredients in oriental cooking which give the food its particular character — garlic and ginger. The Chinese have always used garlic with sparing elegance to create delicately spiced dishes which still delight us today. In India, garlic is used in larger quantities alongside a number of other spices.

This versatile seasoning, one of the oldest known to man, is found in all the great cuisines of the world. It also features world-wide in pharmacopeias. It is certainly one of the most remarkable 'food remedies' that we possess.

The ancient Egyptians thought so highly of garlic that when they took oaths they invoked it as a deity, and even worshipped it; it was so holy that their priests were not allowed to eat it. The slaves who built the pyramid of Cheops were given cloves of garlic to eat every day to keep their strength up, in addition to leeks and onions—to the total value 1,600 talents of silver, which is equivalent to over £1 million today! The Egyptians left whitewashed clay models of garlic in ordinary graves, and six real garlic bulbs were found in the tomb of Tutankhamun, probably put there to keep evil spirits away.

The Greeks and Romans held garlic in high esteem too: their soldiers chewed it in vast quantities to build up their strength, and they nicknamed it 'stinking rose'. Traditionally, Greek athletes would chew a clove of garlic before competing in the Olympic games, and to them it was synonymous with health, energy and longevity. They thought it food fit for a goddess, and placed it ceremoniously on piles of stones at crossroads as an offering to Hecate. The root-gatherers of ancient Greece paid homage to the magic power of garlic by consuming large amounts of it before cutting certain herbs.

In Homer's 'Odyssey', the God Hermes recommends garlic (or moly) to Odysseus as a charm against the sorcery of Circe, and it was this that made her fall passionately in love with him and so escape the fate of his companions, of being turned into a pig.

'Thus while he spoke, the sovereign plant he drew,
Where on th'all-bearing earth unmark'd it grew,
And shewed its nature and its wondrous pow'r;
Black was the root, but milky white the flow'r;
Moly the name, to mortals hard to find,
But all is easy to th'ethereal kind.
This Hermes gave, then gliding off the glade
Shot to Olympus from the woodland shade.'

Odyssey Book X (Transl. Pope)

Garlic was one of the four hundred simples of the Father of Medicine, Hippocrates, who in the 5th century BC discovered its real medicinal and curative properties. Hippocrates also described its toxicity:

'Garlic causes flatulence, a feeling of warmth in the chest and a heavy sensation in the head; it excites anxiety and increases any pain which may be present. Nevertheless, it has the good quality that it increases the secretion of urine.' Galen, Hippocrates' great follower, thought it a panacea and named it 'Heal-all'.

The medicinal powers of garlic were described by the Roman poet Virgil when he told how Thestylis pressed out the juice of wild thyme and garlic and administered it to his reapers as a prophylactic against snake-bites, and Pliny the elder said of garlic that 'taken in wine, it is a remedy for the bite of the shrew-mouse . . . The gashes of garlic mixed with oil, will cure running ulcers of the head.'

Garlic was introduced into Britain by the Romans. In the Dark Ages it was probably only grown in Monastery gardens, disappearing elsewhere, but with the awakening in the Middle Ages and the Anglo-Saxon interest in herbs and simples garlic again became popular. It became known as moly, after Homer's fabulous and magical plant.

'To find a name for me the gods took care
A mystic name that might my worth declare.
They call me Moly: dull grammarian's sense
    is puzzled with the term,
But Homer held divine intelligence.
In Greek and Latin both my name is great
The term is just, but Moly sounds more neat
My powers prevented Circe's dire design;
Ulysses but for me had been a swine.
In vain had Mercury inspired his brain

With craft, and tripped his wheedling tongue in
   vain,
Had I not enter'd timely to his aid.'

The name moly was subsequently applied to
various plants supposed to be identical with Homer's
moly, especially the wild garlic *Allium moly,* a native
of southern Europe and introduced into England in
1597.

Garlic was first cultivated in English gardens in
about 1540 but by Elizabethan times it was thought
of as peasant food. It was commonly known as 'the
poor man's physic, of special value to seafaring men,
because it pacifieth the disposition to vomit.' Bullein,
in his *Book of Simples* of 1562, considered it a gross
form of medicine and most unpleasant for 'fayre
ladyes' who 'prefer sweet breathes before gentle
wordes.'

Its aroma has dogged garlic throughout its history,
and from time immemorial has made it the target for
ribald jokes — and not without reason. Its smell is so
penetrating that even when a clove is rubbed into the
soles of the feet the odour is exhaled by the lungs!

Alphonse, King of Castile in the 14th century,
could not abide the smell and when he instituted an
order of knighthood he had it written into the statutes
that any knight who had eaten garlic was not to come
near him for at least a month! John Evelyn, the
17th century diarist, loathed garlic: 'We absolutely
forbid it entrance into our Salleting by reason of its
intolerable Rankness, and which made it so detested

of old that the eating of it was part of the Punishment for such as had committed the horrid'st Crimes.'

Our recent ancestors therefore regarded it as peasant food, an attitude which has changed fundamentally in modern times. Since World War II travel is no longer the domain of the rich and privileged, and more people than ever before are travelling the world and sampling regional cooking. They have experienced the delights of garlic cooking as offered by the masters of the art — the French, Spanish, Italians — and have brought home to their own kitchens strings of locally grown garlic to cook with themselves. People in northern Europe are beginning to grow their own garlic too, and the few farmers who grow it in this country cannot meet the demand for it in the market place. Garlic is gradually converting the sceptical northerners who have for so long spurned it.

In the United States the popularity of the plant has led to garlic-promotion on a bonanza scale. The annual Garlic Festival held in Gilroy, California, draws crowds of tens of thousands who make merry as only Americans can. They hold the 'Garlic Squeeze Barn Dance', the 'Love That Garlic' tennis tournament, the 'Great Garlic Gallop' and the 'Breathtaking Bicycle Criterium'. They crown a Garlic Queen and there is a Miss Garlic pageant to delight the onlookers. Over 100 food stands compete in the 'Great Garlic Recipe Cook-off' which reeks of over 300 pounds of garlic, and there are contests for garlic-braiding, garlic-topping and garlic-popcorn eating. Bumper stickers proclaim that 'Life without garlic is tasteless', and motorists are helpfully directed:

'Roses are red, garlic is white,
Parking is free, just turn to the right.'

The Garlic Times, published in California, is devoted entirely to garlic news: no gradual conversion this, more of a cult.

The pendulum has swung; garlic is now recognised as the finest of herbs when it is used with discretion and artistry, and the market is flooded with cookery books which describe dishes of the world both great and humble. Today garlic is on the grocery list of every average housewife, whereas twenty years ago you had to search hard and travel far to obtain a bulb. Happily, it has come back into its own: the herb that the Chinese cherished 2000 years ago has re-established its rightful place in our lives.

GARLIC QUOTATIONS

'And, most dear actors, eat no onions or garlic, for we are to utter sweet breath.'

> Shakespeare, *A Midsummer Night's Dream*

'The murmuring Israelites...prized it even before manna itself, some avow it soveraigne for man and beasts in most maladies, though the scent thereof be somewhat valiant and offensive. Indeed a large book is written on its virtues, which if held proportionate with truth, one would wonder any man should die, who hath garlic growing in his garden.'

> Thomas Fuller, 1644

'I have been spending some weeks of dissipation in London, and was transformed by Circe's cup not into a brute but into a beau. I am now eating the herb moly in the country.'

> Sidney Smith, 1813

'That wicked garlic...more poisonous than hemlock... What venom is this that rages in my frame? Has viper's blood without my knowledge been brewed into these herbs?...If ever, my merry Mycaenas, you wish to repeat the jest, I pray your sweetheart may put her hands before your kisses, and lie on the farthest edge of the couch.'

> Horace, Epode 3

GARLIC PRODUCERS

Comparatively little garlic is grown in the UK, and the main crop that is grown here comes from a farm on the Isle of Wight, where 25 acres yield about 30-40 tonnes a year. The climate, and poor light intensity, restrict the yield to a maximum of 2 tonnes per acre. However, this farm supplies major supermarkets throughout the country.

World production of garlic in 1978 was just over 2 million tonnes — the main producers being China, Thailand, Spain and Egypt. Until 1975, Italy was the top garlic growing country in Europe, but a badly diminished crop in 1976 led the way for Spain, Egypt and Argentina to capture her market, and from 1977 they have established their supremacy.

In the USA, garlic is grown almost exclusively in California, near Gilroy, and this area produces 90% of the US crop. There are 14,000 acres turned over to garlic cultivation, which yield 150 million pounds and a $100 million a year industry. Exports go mainly to Canada, Mexico and the West Indies.

HOW TO GET THE BEST OUT OF GARLIC

BUYING GARLIC

Buy heads of garlic that are plump and unbruised, not soft or soggy, and always check that they have not started to dry out. You will be able to tell a great deal just by handling them: if the heads are firm and undented, have no tears in the skin and no discolouration, and are clean, then they will be in good condition. Make sure, too, that they show no signs of mould or external sprouting. Choose heads with regular and reasonable-sized cloves.

STORING GARLIC

Store garlic in a cool dry place away from other vegetables. Allow the air to circulate around the bulbs.

COOKING WITH GARLIC

When cooking with garlic, beware that it does not burn: it singes far more quickly than onions do, and once it is burnt it is quite inedible and smells terrible. It is best to add garlic towards the end of the cooking, particularly when frying, for this reason.

You can transform garlic by boiling it — it loses its sting and becomes a gentle and delicately aromatic vegetable. Cook single, unpeeled cloves for two minutes in boiling water, then cool and peel them. Cook them with the dish that you are preparing — a soup or casserole perhaps — for twenty to thirty minutes. They are delicious and bear no resemblance in taste (or after-effects!) to the uncooked cloves.

EATING IT RAW

Garlic is delicious raw, and to get the best out of it use it as soon as you have prepared it. It is equally good peeled and finely chopped, pounded in a mortar, or crushed in a garlic crusher (which is an essential piece of equipment for those who eat garlic in quantity). The magic about all three methods is that each one succeeds in producing a subtly different taste from

the other. The Spanish put cloves under the kitchen knife and squash them with a sharp blow before they chop — and this gives a different flavour again.

DEHYDRATED GARLIC

Garlic is available commercially in dehydrated form. It can be bought as flakes, pieces, grits and powder. These are useful additions to the larder shelf and can be used for flavouring salad dressings, meat balls, sauces, stews and curries, chutneys and pickles. Garlic salt is also a popular condiment.

In its dehydrated form, garlic is virtually odourless, but when re-hydrated the flavour is almost as good as that of the fresh bulb. Three pounds of fresh garlic yield one pound of dried.

Garlic paste and garlic oil are produced for the food trade and are used to flavour many commercial food products.

HOW TO EAT GARLIC AND STILL SMELL SWEET

One herb and one spice in particular have special affinities with garlic: parsley is the herb and salt the spice. Both bring out the best in garlic. Indeed, parsley is a valuable herb for garlic lovers: chew a sprig of parsley and your breath will no longer reek of garlic!

If the thought of the smell of garlic on your breath deters you from enjoying its pleasures, try this remedy: swallow a clove of garlic, whole, before you embark on your garlic-flavoured meal and your breath will be as sweet-smelling as the breath of the abstainer. And there is good news from Japan, where a farmer has recently developed a strain of odourless garlic. If it has the same flavour, it could revolutionise the market!

The Japanese have also manufactured an odourless garlic powder for those who wish to enjoy the taste without the after-effects. For those people who wish to avoid the smell and yet want to take garlic for its anti-bacterial properties, garlic pearls can be bought from most chemists.

What a shame it is for garlic-eaters to have to worry about such a thing as halitosis — after all, if everyone ate garlic nobody would find it objectionable!

RECIPES FOR
GARLICKY STARTERS
GARLIC SOUP

Because of the long cooking of the garlic cloves, this soup has a soft and subtle flavour. To make it a meal in itself you can garnish it with a poached egg — an excellent lunch!

2 heads of garlic
2 pints of water
a bouquet garni
salt and pepper
3 tablespoons olive oil
2 oz (4 tablespoons) butter
1 oz (¼ cup) flour
2 oz grated parmesan

Drop the separated, unpeeled cloves of garlic into boiling water and boil for 30 seconds. Drain, cool and peel.

Place the garlic, water, herbs, seasonings and olive oil in a saucepan, bring to the boil and simmer for 30 minutes. Then strain the liquid, squeezing the juice out of the garlic with the back of a wooden spoon.

Melt the butter, stir in the flour and gradually pour in the liquid, stirring until it is smooth. Simmer for 5 minutes and serve with the grated parmesan.

For 4

CHINESE DIP FOR SHRIMP

This dip, with its classic combination of garlic and ginger, has a distinct flavour of the Orient, and the soft ribbons of lettuce make it a mouth-watering first course.

3 cloves of garlic, finely sliced
1 teaspoon fresh ginger, shredded
¼ pint (½ cup) vegetable oil
¼ pint (½ cup) soy sauce
1 fresh green chile pepper
1 teaspoon sugar
1 lettuce heart, finely shredded.

Heat the garlic and the ginger gently in the oil for 5 minutes. Add all the other ingredients and mix well.

Heat through and dip 1lb peeled shrimp into the hot mixture, scooping out the ribbons of lettuce to twist, like spaghetti, around them.

For 4

GARLIC AND ANCHOVY FONDUE

A wonderful dish for an informal supper party, it is quickly made, friendly and highly sophisticated. In Italy, they make this dish with olive oil instead of cream, and call it 'bagna cauda' — it is equally irresistible.

2 oz (4 tablespoons) butter
8 anchovy fillets
2 large cloves of garlic, finely chopped
¾ pint (1½ cups) double cream
raw vegetables

Melt the butter over a low heat. Rinse and chop the anchovy fillets very finely, and add to the butter with the garlic. Cook gently for a few minutes.

Heat the cream in the fondue pot, then add the anchovy mixture and stir it in well.

Let the mixture simmer as you serve it with breadsticks and small pieces of raw vegetables — cucumber, cauliflower, carrots, peppers, celery, raw mushrooms and chicory, for example.

For 4

AIOLI WITH CRUDITÉS

Aioli is one of the great classic sauces of France, served with raw vegetables of your choice. (It is sublime with cooked cold asparagus). Aioli is not for the timid — the taste of garlic permeates the mayonnaise and lingers long on the breath.

4 large cloves of garlic
¾ pint (1½ cups) mayonnaise
raw vegetables
bread

Crush the garlic or pound it in a mortar, add it to the mayonnaise (home-made, preferably) and leave in a cool place while you prepare the vegetables.

To the vegetables suggested for the fondue, you could add lightly cooked French beans, spring onions, strips of crisp lettuce, sliced zucchini, either raw or cooked, and cubes of cold boiled beetroot.

Serve the aioli with crudités and little squares of fresh bread, and a bottle of lusty red wine.

For 4

SKORDALIA

Skordalia is a traditional Greek hors-d'oeuvre. The recipe may look bland and unappetising on paper, but the dish is extraordinarily delicious for all its simplicity, once the mixture has been left to soften.

a 2-inch slice of bread
2 large cloves of garlic
1/3 pint (2/3 cup) olive oil
lemon juice
salt
water

Cut the crusts off the bread and soak it in water for 2 minutes, then squeeze it dry.

Pound the garlic in a mortar until it is quite crushed, and add the bread. Pound the bread and the garlic in the mortar until the two are well-amalgamated. Gradually add the olive oil in a slow stream of drips, as if you were making mayonnaise. Add lemon juice and salt to taste. When well-mixed, add a little cold water and stir until smooth. Leave to stand and soften for several hours, or overnight.

Serve the skordalia with pitta bread, or dish it up with sliced root vegetables such as beetroot, baby turnips and radishes. It is equally good simply served with tomatoes, olives and hard-boiled eggs. For a main course, serve it with fried fish, or with fried aubergines (eggplant) and zucchini.

SOME MAIN COURSES

GARLIC OMELETTE

This is a useful standby if you need to prepare something quick and delicious — and a bit different at the same time.

2 slices of white bread
2 oz (4 tablespoons) butter
1 large clove of garlic, crushed
4 tablespoons chopped parsley
8 eggs
cream or milk
salt and pepper

Cut the crusts off the bread and cut into small squares. Melt the butter in a pan over a gentle heat and cook the bread squares in it until they are golden and crisp all over. Add the garlic and parsley and set to one side.

Make your omelette in the usual way with the eggs, cream or milk, and seasonings, and use the garlic croûtons as a filling.

Serve with a crisp green salad.

For 4

You can also use these garlic croûtons as a special garnish for buttered or creamed spinach.

GARLIC TOPS WITH EGGS

This recipe comes from India, where they eat it once a year to give them 'heat' for the rest of the year — the Indian answer to central heating! Serve it in May or early June when the tops of the garlic growing in the garden (or in a pot) are young and green. They are quite delicious, and the eggs turn out like softly coddled eggs.

3 garlic tops per person
2 eggs per person
2 oz (4 tablespoons) butter per person

Chop the garlic leaves finely and put them on to a very hot ovenproof dish. Heat the butter until it is sizzling and frothy. Break the eggs over the leaves and then pour over the sizzling hot butter so that it cooks the eggs. Let the whites begin to set before you start to eat — and then eat it up quickly before it has time to get cold.

This simple dish, served with a mixture of spiced rice and mung beans sprinkled with chopped coriander, is a veritable feast.

PIPERADE

This wonderful luncheon dish comes from the Basque country. It is rugged and strong, its flavours linger on the palate leaving echoes of its native countryside.

3 green peppers
1 lb tomatoes
1 tablespoon olive oil
2 cloves of garlic
basil
salt and pepper
2 eggs, well beaten
croûtons of fried bread

Cut the peppers into strips, and peel and chop the tomatoes.

Heat the oil in a large pan and cook the peppers for about 10 minutes. Add the tomatoes, garlic, basil and seasonings and cook until the tomatoes are pulpy. Stir in the eggs, stirring until they begin to scramble.

Serve on hot plates with the croûtons and a green salad.

For 2

SPAGHETTI WITH GARLIC AND OLIVE OIL

Thoroughly Italian, entirely easy, and unspeakably delicious! Many pasta experts swear that this is the best sauce in the world for spaghetti, and plenty of Italians certainly think so. In essence, cast caution to the winds and dress as much spaghetti as you can eat with good olive oil, a little salt, masses of crushed garlic and freshly ground black pepper. It needs nothing to go with it bar a good rustic red wine.

PASTA PESTO

This famous Italian sauce is made with pine nuts in its native country, but since they are not widely available, you can use walnuts instead.

1 large bunch of basil
2 large cloves of garlic, peeled
4 oz walnuts
¼ pint (½ cup) olive oil
2 oz grated parmesan

Put the basil, garlic, nuts and oil in a blender and blend thoroughly. Stir in the parmesan.

Store the pesto sauce in screw-top jars in the refrigerator throughout the summer and serve it with freshly-cooked pasta. Alternatively, try serving it on baked mushrooms, or with cauliflower, or as a sauce for white fish.

PRAWNS WITH GARLIC AND GINGER

A seductive dish for dining à deux. It tastes exotic, is effortless to make, and has all the finesse and simplicity which is the magic of Chinese cookery.

1 large clove of garlic, finely chopped
1 oz green ginger, finely chopped
2 shallots, finely chopped
olive oil
8 oz large shelled prawns (shrimp)
salt and pepper
sugar
3 to 4 tablespoons cream

Fry the garlic, ginger and shallots very gently in oil until they are soft, taking care not to overheat. Add the prawns and turn up the heat a little. Cook for 2 minutes. Season with salt, pepper and add a pinch of sugar.

Stir in the cream, heat through, and serve with egg noodles.

For 2

COD CUTLETS WITH QUICK GARLIC SAUCE

This sauce is an ideal accompaniment to fresh white fish and makes a pleasant change from more traditional sauces. Serve this dish with new potatoes and broccoli.

4 cod cutlets
butter

For the sauce
1 oz flaked almonds
2 large cloves of garlic
½ pint (1 cup) stock
2 oz (½ cup) breadcrumbs
cream

To make the sauce, blend all the sauce ingredients in a blender and then stir over a gentle heat for 10 minutes. Finish with a little cream.

Grill or fry the cod cutlets in butter until cooked, and serve with the garlic sauce.

You can equally well serve the sauce with other fish — for example whiting, plaice, eel or mackerel.

For 4

CHICKEN WITH GARLIC

The whole cloves of garlic baked slowly inside the chicken give it a delicious aroma and a unique taste. Garlic lovers can chew the softened cloves!

2 heads of garlic
3lb chicken
2 oz (4 tablespoons) butter
salt and pepper

Peel the cloves of garlic and put them inside the cavity of the chicken, along with half of the butter. Season the skin all over with salt and pepper and place upside down in a baking dish. Sliver the rest of the butter and put it all over the chicken.

Bake at 325°F, 160°C, gas 3 for 2 hours, turning the chicken the right way up for the last 30 minutes.

Serve with the juices from the pan, and new potatoes.

For 4

GREEK GARLIC PORK

This recipe comes from a remote village in Crete and conjures up azure skies, breathless heat, and Sunday lunch in the shade of olive trees.

1 leg of pork
salt
1 head of garlic
8 oz each of carrots, celery and onions
olive oil
salt and pepper
stock and white wine

Season the pork all over with salt, and lard lavishly with pieces of garlic.

Slice the vegetables and cook in olive oil until they are softened. Season with salt and pepper.

Put the vegetables into a large casserole, place the pork on top and pour over enough white wine and stock to cover the vegetables. Cook at 325°F, 160°C, gas 3 for 45 minutes per pound.

Serve with a Greek salad and a bottle or two of retsina.

For 6

PORK WITH MUSSELS

This recipe comes from Portugal. Traditionally, they make it with clams, but mussels are a good substitute

1 lb fillet or pork
1 large glass of dry sherry
2 heaped teaspoons paprika
1 bay leaf
2 cloves
salt and pepper
3 cloves of garlic, crushed
2 large onions
olive oil
4 tomatoes
2 cloves of garlic, crushed
1 lb frozen mussels
chopped parsley
1 lemon

Cut the pork into small cubes and put into a bowl. Pour over the sherry and add the paprika, bay leaf, cloves and seasonings. Add the garlic and leave to marinate for several hours.

Slice the onions and cook them very gently in olive oil until they are soft. Peel and chop the tomatoes and add them with the garlic to the onions and cook until well heated through. Add the mussels and the chopped parsley.

Meanwhile, drain the pork and keep the marinade. Fry the meat in hot olive oil until well browned. Add the marinade and cook until it is well reduced. Add to the onion and mussel mixture, and serve garnished with lemon quarters.

For 4

KOREAN FILLET STEAKS

The Koreans have an exquisite way of treating and eating steak — the marinade permeates the slivers of meat and softens them at the same time. Get your butcher to cut really thin slices, the thinner the better.

soy sauce
sugar
3 cloves of garlic per person, crushed.
2 thin slices of fillet steak per person

Make a marinade with soy sauce, sugar and crushed garlic. Let the beef slices stand in it for 3-4 hours, then wipe them clean.

Cook fleetingly, either over a very hot barbecue or in sizzling hot olive oil, for only a few seconds on each side.

Serve with fried aubergines (eggplant), spiced rice and salad.

GARLIC WITH
VEGETABLES

GARLIC MUSHROOMS

Garlic and mushrooms have a special relationship,
the herb seems to bring out the best in the flavour of
the mushroom, and together they form a sophisticated team.

1 very large mushroom per person
½ small bread roll per person
butter
chopped parsley
garlic to taste
grated parmesan

Season the mushroom caps and place them, without
their stalks, in an ovenproof dish. Cover with foil and
bake at 350°F, 180°C, gas 4 for 15-20 minutes.
Hollow out the rolls and cook them for 10 minutes so
that they are crisp.

Meanwhile, chop the mushroom stalks and cook
them in butter with the chopped parsley. Add the
crushed garlic and warm through for a minute.

Slip the baked mushrooms into the hollowed-out
rolls, fill with garlicky stuffing and serve immediately
with grated parmesan.

LIMA BEAN AND
GARLIC SALAD

This salad comes from Israel. It is appetisingly light and makes a pretty addition to a cold buffet table.

8 oz lima beans
1 large clove of garlic
1 small carton plain yogurt
lemon juice
salt
chopped parsley
chopped dill

Cook the beans lightly in salted water and allow to cool.

Crush the garlic into the yogurt and season with lemon juice, salt, and chopped parsley and dill. Mix in the beans and serve chilled.

For 4

GARLIC POTATOES

The flavour of cooked garlic makes a world of difference to mashed potatoes, especially deep into the winter months when old potatoes are discouragingly same-ish. This is the way to transform your daily fare!

2 heads of garlic
2 oz (4 tablespoons) butter
1 lb mashed potatoes
cream and more butter
salt and pepper
2 tablespoons chopped parsley

Boil the whole heads of garlic for 2 minutes, and then drain, cool and peel the cloves. Melt the butter and cook the garlic gently until it is tender but not browned. Sieve it.

Add the sieved garlic to the mashed potatoes, mix well and then add cream, butter, seasonings and chopped parsley. Heat through and serve.

For 4

HUNGARIAN CABBAGE AND RICE

This is an interesting mid-European dish which has a characteristic Hungarian feel to it. Its virtue lies in the fact that it is a complete accompaniment. It is particularly good served with roast pork and gravy.

1 lb cabbage
8 oz rice
4 oz bacon, in a piece
vegetable oil
1 large onion, finely sliced
3 cloves of garlic, crushed
3 eggs
1 small carton sour cream
salt and pepper
2 oz (½ cup) breadcrumbs
4 oz grated cheese

Cut the cabbage into cubes and cook in boiling water for 2-3 minutes and drain. Boil the rice. Cut the bacon into cubes and cook in vegetable oil with the onion until the latter is softened. Add the garlic.

Separate the eggs and beat the whites until they are stiff. Beat the yolks and add the sour cream, then fold into the whites. Add the cabbage, rice and the bacon mixture to the eggs, mix well and season to taste.

Pour the mixture into a greased baking dish, mix the breadcrumbs with cheese and sprinkle over the top. Bake at 400°F, 200°C, gas 6 for 30 minutes.

For 6

AUBERGINES IMAM BAYELDI

A famous favourite from Turkey, there are varying stories about how this dish got its name — which means 'the Imam fainted'. The most colourful one relates how an Imam, a Turkish priest, fainted with pleasure when these stuffed aubergines (eggplants) were served up to him by his wife. Another tells how he fainted when he heard how much precious olive oil went into the dish! However the aubergines got their name, they make a delicious first course, or a simple supper dish served with salad.

1 medium aubergine (eggplant)
salt
8 oz (1½ cups) onions, finely sliced
olive oil
3 large cloves of garlic, finely sliced
8 oz (1 cup) tomatoes, peeled and chopped
bunch of parsley, chopped
salt and pepper
juice of 1 lemon

Cut the aubergine into half lengthwise, and remove the seeds to make a cavity. Sprinkle the cut edges with salt and leave for 30 minutes to sweat. Wipe dry.

Meanwhile, cook the onions gently in olive oil until they are soft. Stir in the garlic and cook for a few minutes longer. Add the peeled and chopped tomatoes and the chopped parsley and stir for a minute or two. Season to taste with salt and pepper, then add the lemon juice.

Fill the aubergine halves with this mixture and put into a baking dish. Pour ¼ inch hot water into the bottom of the dish and bake at 350°F, 180°C, gas 4 for 1 hour.

Leave to cool and serve cold.

For 2

◆

SOME GARLIC GOODIES

GARLIC BREAD

A famous recipe which never fails to delight. Garlic bread brings out the greedy instinct in everyone.

2 large cloves of garlic
salt
4 oz butter
1 French loaf

Crush the garlic, add a little salt and stir into melted butter. Cool and leave to set.

Slice the bread and spread both sides with the butter. Reconstitute the loaf on a piece of foil, wrap it up firmly and bake for 10 minutes at 400°F, 200°C, gas 6.

GARLIC BUTTER

For all its simplicity, this is one of the most delicious butters in the world.

4 oz butter
2 large cloves of garlic, crushed
a small bunch of parsley, very finely chopped

Melt the butter and stir in the crushed garlic. Stir over a low heat for a few minutes and then add the chopped parsley. Continue to stir over the heat for a few minutes until the parsley has wilted. Put the butter into a container to set.

FOR THE LARDER

GARLIC OIL

Crush garlic to taste into good olive oil. Leave to stand for a minimum of 30 minutes, and use on salads instead of vinaigrette.

For a more gently-flavoured garlic oil to use in cooking and in a vinaigrette, you can make this oil: to every pint of oil add ½ oz (1 tablespoon) chopped garlic. Leave to stand for a few days, shaking occasionally, and it will then be ready to use.

GARLIC VINEGAR

3 large cloves of garlic
¾ pint (1½ cups) white wine vinegar

Peel the garlic and chop it coarsely, then crush the pieces in a mortar.

Heat half of the vinegar to boiling point and pour it on to the garlic. Cool, and then add the rest of the vinegar and decant it into a bottle.

Leave for 2 weeks, shaking daily, and then strain and re-bottle.

GARLIC OLIVES

This idea originated in Spain, and has become very popular in France; it deserves to cross the water. Garlic transforms olives and makes delectable morsels to nibble with pre-dinner drinks.

garlic
black olives
olive oil

Lightly bruise several cloves of garlic in a mortar.

Pack the olives into a screw-top jar with the garlic. Pour olive oil over the olives so that they are covered, screw down and store for several days before using. Garlic olives keep indefinitely.

NUTRITIONAL VALUE

A clove of garlic is made up of minute quantities of water, fat, sugars, cellulose, pectin, mucilage, total ash, acid soluble ash, peptides and proteins. It also contains certain minerals, including sodium, iodine, potassium, iron, calcium, phosphorus, sulphur, zinc, nitrogen, cobalt, chromium, magnesium and copper. Vitamins A, B_1 and B_3, and C are present, and each clove contains between 5 and 7 calories.

HEALTH AND MEDICINE

'This herbe allium is called Garlecke. The vertue of this herbe is thus: It will unbynde all wycked wyndes within a mannes body. Also it helpeth a man to make water. But it noyeth a mannes eyes bycause of ye great byndynge and drynkynge that it hath vertuously. It drynketh and destroyeth the syght. And also it destroyeth and heleth venym within a man. Also it heleth cold soores and marfewes or bladders in what maner place they be in a mannes body, so that it be well froted therewith. The herbe is hote and dry.'

Thus wrote Richard Banckes in his herbal of 1525, well before garlic's place in medicine had been established.

Garlic contains only 0.1% essential oil, but this oil contains the anti-bacterial substance allicin, which is also responsible for garlic's characteristic smell. Allicin is found in the bulb; it has antiseptic qualities, is an expectorant and an intestinal antispasmodic. Herbal physicians have prescribed garlic for their patients for centuries, and medical science today is increasingly interested in its curative powers.

Garlic has been found to be extremely effective used externally as an antiseptic. During World War I, surgeons who had to operate on wounded soldiers without supplies of conventional antiseptics used garlic juice on swabs of sphagnum moss to prevent the wounds from going septic, and, in 1916, the British government were offering one shilling per pound for as many tons of garlic as could be produced.

Garlic oil, rubbed into the skin, is a good insect repellent — if you can tolerate it as your perfume! This oil is rich in both iodine and sulphur, which are necessary for the healthy balance of the thyroid gland, and the pharmaceutical industry manufactures several products using garlic oil. It is also believed to be prophylactic in occupational and chronic lead poisoning. In veterinary medicine, garlic oil is used to expel ticks, and it is used in a preparation for treating foot-and-mouth disease.

Garlic has found its way into folk medicine, too. A swab of garlic is a country remedy for a nosebleed, and garlic's antimicrobial properties are thought to make eating it an efficient way of getting rid of worms.

Many people believe that garlic affords protection against the common cold, sore throats, amoebic dysentery and other infectious diseases, thanks to its power to destroy dangerous germs. Its history is full of medical success stories. It was the main ingredient in the 'Four Thieves' Vinegar', a remedy used during an outbreak of the plague in Marseilles in 1722, when four convicted thieves maintained that eating garlic had protected them from infection while they were robbing the dead bodies of victims of the epidemic. This protective property of the garlic bulb is supported by another historical anecdote. During an outbreak of infectious fever in some London slums in the early 19th century, French priests, who ate garlic at every meal, were able to minister to the sick with no hazard to their health, whereas the English non-garlic-eating clergy caught the infection. Garlic was for a long time used in the treatment of leprosy, and lepers even acquired the nickname 'pilgarlic', from the fact that they were made to peel garlic for their own consumption. As early as 1758, garlic's healing capacity was recorded in a cholera outbreak — and when later cholera epidemics struck, people used to clutch garlic cloves for salvation.

Garlic is an expectorant and is therefore good for treating asthma, bronchitis and catarrh, usually in the form of a syrup. In catarrhal pneumonia bruised garlic cloves used to be applied as a poultice to the chest and they acted as a counter-irritant by being absorbed through the skin.

Garlic has at one time or another been made into a liniment for rheumatic pains and neuritis, and bruised cloves mixed with lard used as an ointment for whooping cough. The ancient Greeks recommended it for clearing the voice, and 5th century Indian physicians followed suit. Pliny names 61 ailments that could be cured by the use of garlic, and Culpeper went as far as to say that it was a remedy for *all* diseases!

This pungent plant is well-known for 'being good for the blood', and it has been found that garlic dilates the blood vessels and is effective in bringing down high blood pressure. It was also shown in 1973 that the garlic juice reduces the blood sugar level in diabetic patients. Fatty particles in the bloodstream are destroyed by the juice, inhibiting the increase of cholesterol in the blood, thus making garlic valuable in the treatment of arteriosclerosis. Research is currently being carried out into the use of garlic in the prevention and treatment of coronary heart disease, and also of cancer. Perhaps it is significant that the Italians, who eat garlic with almost everything, have a lower incidence of heart disease than any other European people—and it is also not without interest that garlic comes from central Asia where people live longer than they do anywhere else in the world, and where they also have the lowest rate of cancer.

Garlic is a general tonic: it stimulates energy and is a diuretic and carminative (which means that it expels air), it keeps the lining of the stomach in good condition and is well-known for aiding digestion and food-absorption. Garlic is also thought to clear the complexion, and Culpeper wrote that 'Garlic takes away spots and blemishes in the skin'. In addition to all this, garlic is an effective remedy for constipation and it is even claimed that it will stop you from growing old — it holds the secret to long life!

FOLK REMEDIES

The lotions and potions given below are based on folk medicines and old wives' tales. Garlic is generally acknowledged to be an effective tonic and aid to digestion, to be an expectorant and to have antiseptic qualities, but you should not attempt to use garlic medicines without first consulting your doctor.

GARLIC LOTION FOR BITES AND STINGS

Crush 2 cloves of garlic and mix with ¼ pint (½ cup) of warm water. Dab on the affected parts.

GARLIC POULTICE FOR SWELLINGS AND INFECTIONS

Crush 1 clove of garlic on to a clean piece of gauze or muslin and cover with another piece of same size. Rub a little oil or cream into the swelling or infected area and lay the poultice on top. Leave it in place until the swelling goes down.

GARLIC POTION FOR GENERAL HEALTH

4 tablespoons milk
1 clove of garlic

Warm the milk, and peel and crush the garlic into a cup. Pour the milk over it, leave to stand for a few minutes and then drink it all down. If you prefer a savoury potion, use consommé instead of milk.

GARLIC LOTION FOR PIMPLES AND BOILS

2 oz (4 tablespoons) lard
2 cloves of garlic

Soften the lard and crush the garlic. Mix the garlic into the lard with a fork until well-blended. Apply directly to the affected areas.

If you have pimples on your face, it is best to eat garlic for its blood-cleansing action rather than risk getting the lotion too near the eyes as it can sting and make them water.

GARLIC COUGH MIXTURE

1 clove of garlic
2 tablespoons honey or syrup

Crush the garlic into the honey or syrup. Take 1 tablespoon twice a day.

GARLIC NOSEBLEED REMEDY

a small piece of gauze
vinegar
2 cloves of garlic

Soak the gauze in the vinegar and then squeeze the juice from the garlic on the gauze, using a garlic crusher. Roll the gauze into a plug and place it in the bleeding nostril. Have a handkerchief handy because your eyes will water!

GARLIC SYRUP FOR
CHEST COMPLAINTS

3 whole heads of garlic
1 pint water
½ pint cider vinegar
2 oz (¼ cup) sugar

Peel all the cloves of garlic, and simmer them gently in the water for 20 minutes. Remove the garlic and put into a jar. Add the vinegar and sugar to the water and boil until reduced to a syrup. Pour it over the garlic cloves in the jar, and cool.

Take one or two of the garlic cloves with the syrup every morning.

GARLIC INSECT SPRAY

2 large cloves of garlic
1 pint water

Peel the cloves and crush them. Heat the water gently and add the garlic, removing the pan from the heat before it reaches the boil. Leave to cool, and spray on to plants affected by onion-fly or aphids.

THE FOLKLORE OF GARLIC

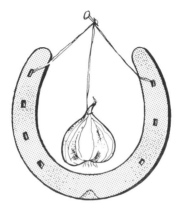

'When Satan stepped out of the Garden of Eden after the fall of man, garlic sprang up from the spot where he placed his left foot, and onion from where his right foot touched the ground.' This Mohammedan saying — from which we can deduce that the Mohammedans didn't think much of garlic— is one of the earliest pieces of garlic lore, and ever since that time legends and magic, old wives' tales and superstitions have grown up around garlic. Being so powerful a medicine, and such unique flavouring for food, it has been closely involved in the everyday life of country people and so the richness of its folklore is hardly surprising.

GARLIC AND MAGIC

Powerful in taste and smell, garlic was thought to be potent in mystical ways as well.

* Garlic's magical powers make it a protection against witchcraft.

* In the Far and Middle East garlic was carried as a talisman. In Chinese mythology, garlic is a ruse against the Evil Eye.

* Put garlic into a baby's cradle to thwart the wicked fairy folk who wish to steal the child and leave a changeling.

* Hang garlic by the kitchen door to keep fairies away from the butter churn.

GARLIC AND DREAM-LORE

One wonders which old wives got together to interpret the meaning of dreaming about garlic, which could hardly have been a common occurrence. They have come up with these two — slightly contradictory — sayings.

* If you dream of garlic you will discover hidden secrets or treasure, and this will lead to domestic strife.

* It is lucky to dream that you have garlic in the house.

GARLIC AND DOGS

'Madde dogges' feature frequently in the great herbals of the 16th and 17th centuries; evidently rabies was common, and so were the ideas for curing it.

*'Against mad dogs: boil all together bruised rue leaves, garlic, Venice treacle and pewter scraping in strong ale. Take 9 spoonsful before food on 7 mornings in a row, and give 6 spoonsful to a bitten dog. Also strain and put the mixture directly on the wound'. This remedy comes from a manuscript dated 1752 found in Calthorpe Church in Lincolnshire. According to the record, a mad dog bit most of the inhabitants in the village and only those who did not take the mixture died.

*To worm a dog, put an unpeeled clove of garlic into its food.

GARLIC AND VAMPIRES

Those cognisant of the desires and phobias of Count Dracula and his ilk will know full well that garlic was the only protection against their evil doings.

*A necklace of garlic keeps vampires away.

*In the Middle Ages, garlic was highly valued for its power to keep vampires at bay.

* In Stoke-on-Trent in 1973, a Pole who had a phobia of vampires attacking him while he slept, died from inhaling a whole clove of garlic in his sleep. Garlic was found in the corners of his room.

GARLIC: OLD WIVES' TALES

The old wives were kept busy over garlic: its truly medicinal properties were extended into the realms of folk medicine, and spilled over into the treatment of animals and birds. Many of these beliefs echo back to ancient Greece where garlic was chewed by athletes for strength and stamina. Quaint as they are, perhaps these sayings contain grains of truth since they have lasted for so many centuries.

*If you hold garlic in the palm of your hand it will cure toothache.

*In Kent, they used to put garlic inside the stockings of a child with the whooping cough in order to cure the complaint; in other parts of England, they put wild garlic into their shoes to help the sufferer.

*Hungarian jockeys sometimes fastened a clove of garlic to the bits of their horses, believing that other races would be kept back by the offensive smell.

*Rub your lips and nose with garlic when working in the fields in hot sunshine, and it will keep off the heat of the sun.

*Pieces of garlic scattered amongst grain helps to keep weevils away.

*If your garden is infested with moles, garlic or leeks will make them 'leap out of the ground presently'.

*Garlic was put into the mash of fighting cocks to give them strength and stamina, and was also mixed into the food of racehorses.

* Chickens lay better eggs if they have garlic put into their feed before they start laying; but once they do start, the garlic must be stopped or it will flavour the eggs.

*Rub your corns with crushed garlic, or put a sliver on the corn and cover it with a bandage. Replace daily for 8-10 days until the corn falls off.

*To cure measles: tear a piece of homespun linen into 9 pieces and spread each one with the powdered garlic from 9 bulbs. Wrap each piece around the child and nurse it for 9 days. Bury the linen in the garden and the child will be cured.

*To cure smallpox: cut garlic into small pieces and apply them to the soles of the feet in a linen cloth. Renew daily.

*If crows eat Crow Garlic is stupifies them.

*Put necklaces of garlic around children's necks to get rid of worms.

*Breathing in the fumes of freshly-crushed garlic bulbs is a useful cure for a fit of hysteria.

ACKNOWLEDGEMENTS

The Fresh Fruit and Vegetable Information Bureau,
   London
Lynne Burbage, The Tropical Products Institute,
   London
The French Embassy, London
Food and Wine from France, London
Italian Trade Centre, London